Lawyers Uncovered

Lawyers Uncovered

Everything you always wanted to know, but
didn't want to pay £500 an hour to find out

Alex Steuart Williams
and Graham Francis Defries

BOOKS

First published in Great Britain in 2007 by JR Books,
10 Greenland Street, London NW1 0ND www.jrbooks.co.uk

A catalogue record for this book is available from the British Library.

ISBN 978 1 906217 08 2

1 3 5 7 9 10 8 6 4 2

Printed by the Cromwell Press Ltd., Trowbridge.

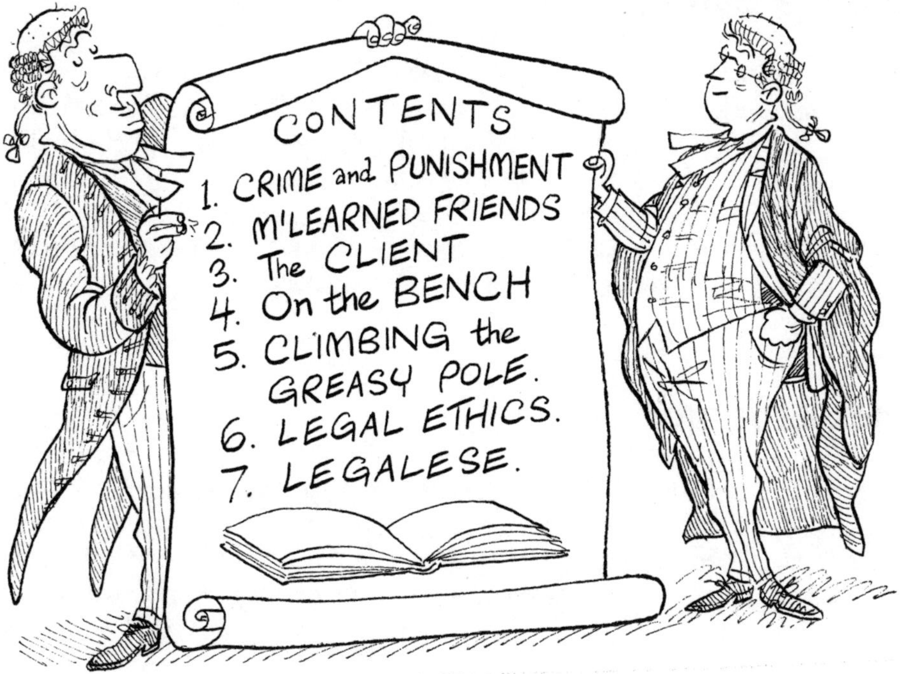
CONTENTS
1. CRIME and PUNISHMENT
2. M'LEARNED FRIENDS
3. The CLIENT
4. On the BENCH
5. CLIMBING the GREASY POLE.
6. LEGAL ETHICS.
7. LEGALESE.

About the authors

Alex Steuart Williams is a former barrister turned cartoonist and feature film animator. His movie credits include *Who Framed Roger Rabbit?*, *The Lion King*, *The Iron Giant* and *Robots*. He is currently living in Jerusalem, where he is directing the forthcoming animated film *The Wild Bunch*.

Graham Francis Defries is a solicitor and partner in the firm of Dechert LLP. He lives in London with his family. Graham specialises in Intellectual property law and poking fun at his partners.

Acknowledgements

The Queen's Counsel cartoon strip has been running in the law pages of *The Times* since October 1993. Since then a number of people have contributed ideas, but none more than Mark Furber, an excellent solicitor and, lately, source of endless material for the strip. Many of the jokes in here are his – including the jacket design. Thank you Mark.

Queen's Counsel Original drawings and prints can be purchased at absurdly reasonable prices at www.qccartoon.com

Introduction by Julian Fellowes

In Charles Dickens's *Oliver Twist*, Mr. Brownlow is obliged to explain to Mr. Bumble that, in a case of petty theft, the law finds him guiltier than Mrs. Bumble, though they acted in tandem, 'for the law supposes that your wife acts under your direction.' 'If the Law supposes *that*,' replies Mr Bumble, 'then the law is a ass.' The notion that a wife is under her husband's control, was a ludicrous presumption even to the mid-Victorians, and it would be lovely to feel that, in the subsequent century and a half, such inanities had been swept away by a reassuring and overdue revival of Common Sense. Sadly (for us, mortals), the Law remains a curious and unpredictable beast, certainly when glimpsed through the pages of the popular press. Here, every day, judgements are reported that seem to fly in the face of all human logic – or at least, what passes for logic in the outside world. But of course the Law and the Real World are two different places, and this is precisely what Steuart and Francis explore and expose to such hilarious, and merciless effect. They understand the bewildering culture of our Courts, inviting us, in the best traditions of Gillray and Rowlandson and all those others who use laughter as a righteous scourge, to view and judge the foreign country that is the British legal system. If most of their jokes look uncomfortably like documentary truth, nevertheless, in *Lawyers Uncovered*, they have provided us with a marvellous tour guide.

Julian Fellowes

Inside the Legal Mind

LITIGATION
HUBRIS
NEMESIS
BLAME
BUCK-PASSING
NEGOTIATION
POMPOSITY
HALF-TRUTHS
GREED
AMBITION
BOREDOM
ENVY
RECREATION
GOLF
OPERA
WINE
FEAR
PRO BONO

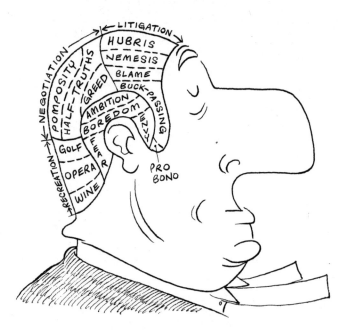

Chapter 1
Crime & Punishment

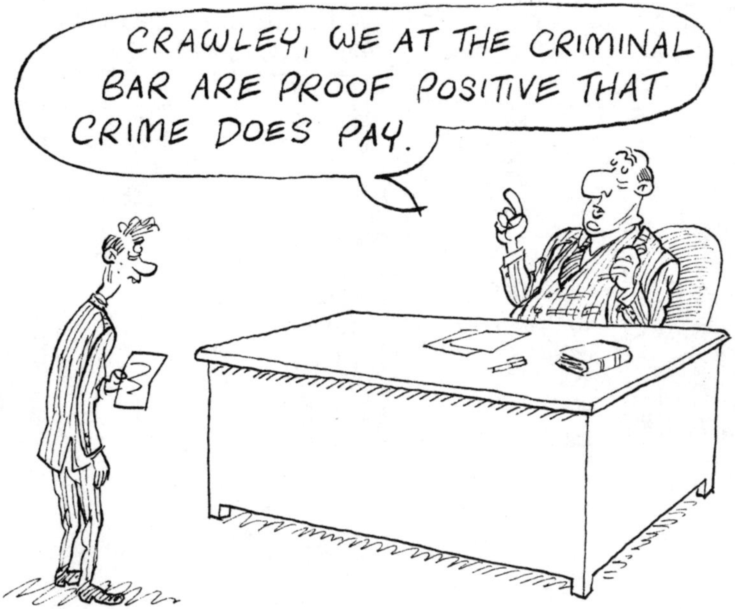
CRAWLEY, WE AT THE CRIMINAL BAR ARE PROOF POSITIVE THAT CRIME DOES PAY.

M'LUD, I SUBMIT THAT A CUSTODIAL SENTENCE WOULD BE INAPPROPRIATE IN THIS CASE
WHAT MY CLIENT NEEDS IS A GOOD FLOGGING
THE DEFENDANT WAS LED ASTRAY BY AN OLDER CRIMINAL FRATERNITY.
HIS FATHER, GRANDFATHER, AND OLDER BROTHER MAKE UP THE FAMILY FIRM
...BUT HE HAS CLOSE TIES WITH THE LOCAL COMMUNITY...
THE POLICE ALL KNOW HIM BY NAME
... AND HE IS VERY SORRY AND WANTS TO BE GIVEN A SECOND CHANCE
...TO STEAL AGAIN AND NOT GET CAUGHT NEXT TIME

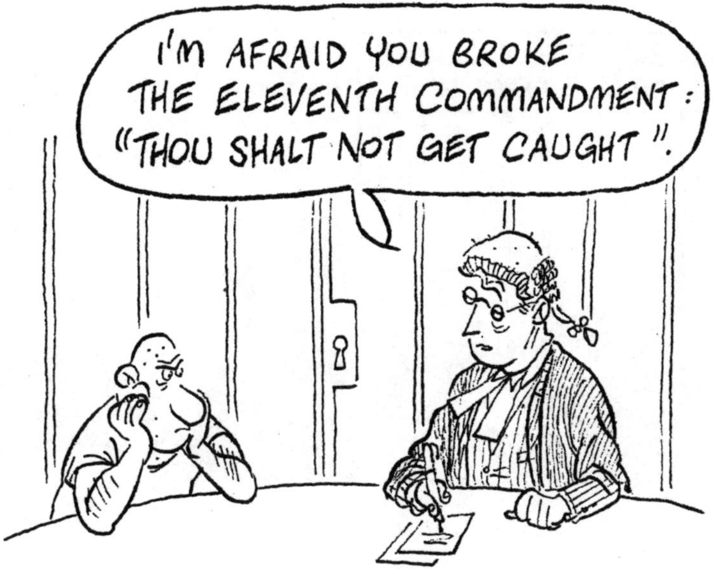
I'M AFRAID YOU BROKE THE ELEVENTH COMMANDMENT: "THOU SHALT NOT GET CAUGHT".

GUILTY! I CAN'T BELIEVE IT! I... I'M STUNNED!
WE DID OUR BEST FOR YOU
YOU NEVER CAN TELL WHAT A JURY WILL DO WITH A CASE LIKE THIS.
BUT... I MEAN... WHERE DO WE GO FROM HERE?
WELL, WE GO BACK TO CHAMBERS
...AND YOU GO TO JAIL

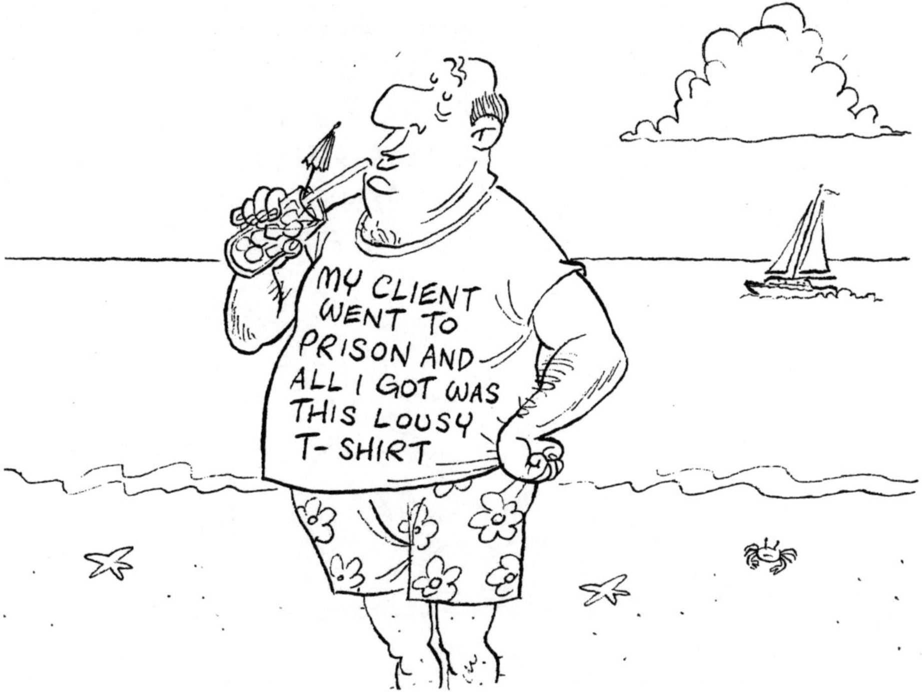
MY CLIENT WENT TO PRISON AND ALL I GOT WAS THIS LOUSY T-SHIRT

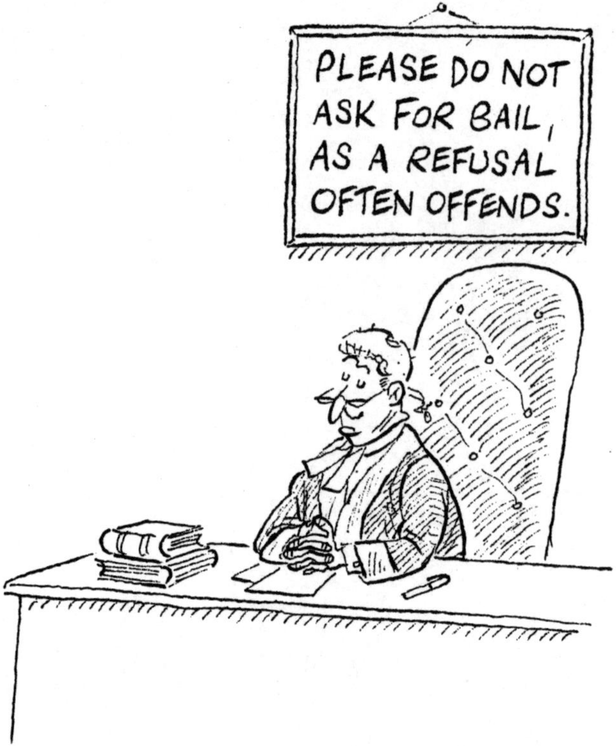
PLEASE DO NOT
ASK FOR BAIL,
AS A REFUSAL
OFTEN OFFENDS.

GOT ANY INTERESTING CASES, SIR GEOFFREY?
JUST THE USUAL GANG OF WEALTHY VILLAINS IN A GOOD DEAL OF TROUBLE.
I ALWAYS TELL THEM THEY'LL NEVER GO TO PRISON WITH ALL THAT MONEY.
...AND IT'S TRUE.
...BY THE TIME THEY GO TO PRISON, THEY'RE FLAT BROKE.

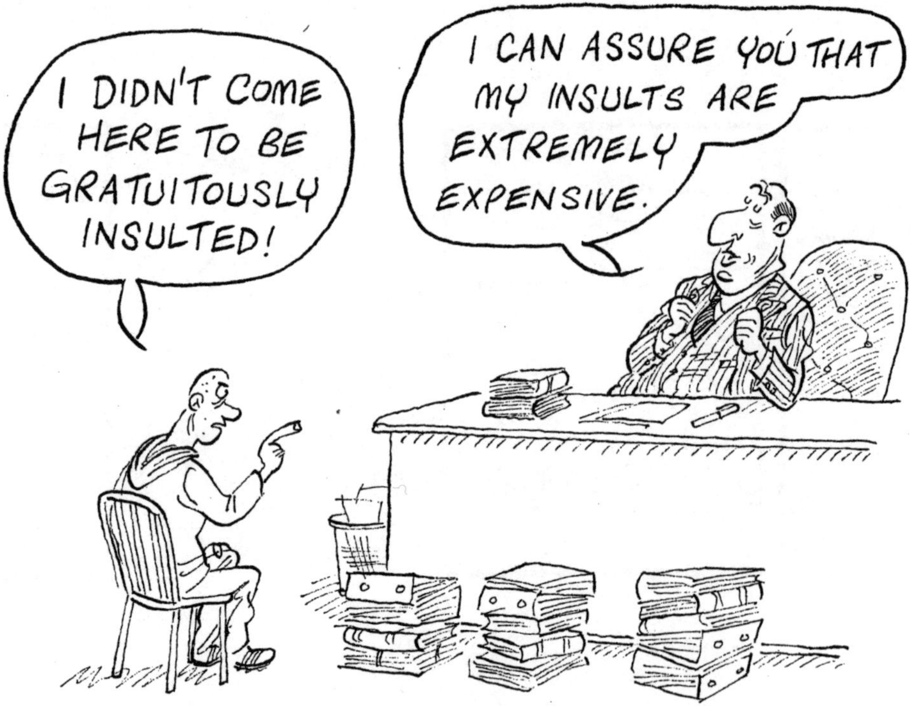
I DIDN'T COME HERE TO BE GRATUITOUSLY INSULTED!
I CAN ASSURE YOU THAT MY INSULTS ARE EXTREMELY EXPENSIVE.

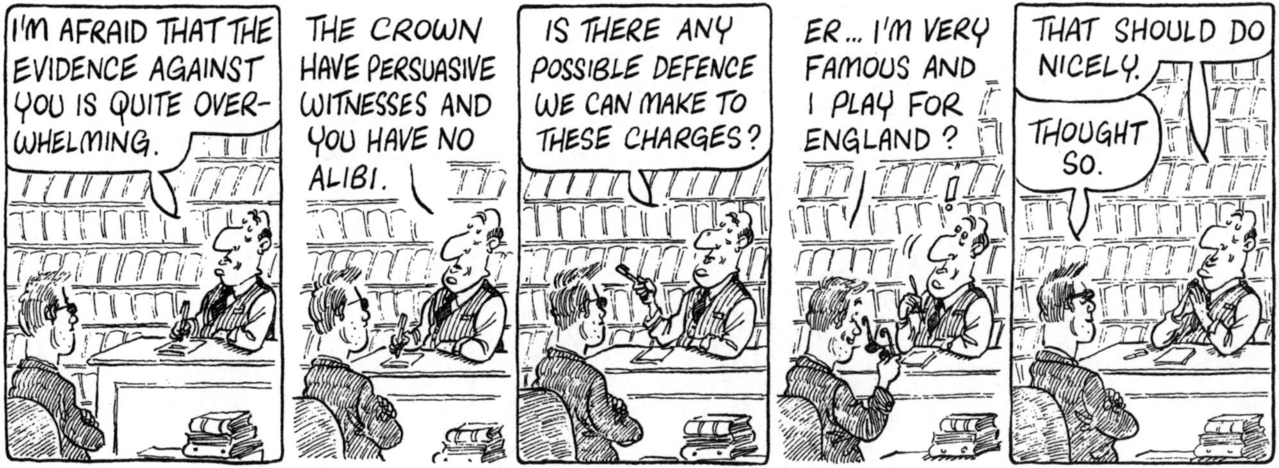

I'M AFRAID THAT THE EVIDENCE AGAINST YOU IS QUITE OVER-WHELMING.
THE CROWN HAVE PERSUASIVE WITNESSES AND YOU HAVE NO ALIBI.
IS THERE ANY POSSIBLE DEFENCE WE CAN MAKE TO THESE CHARGES?
ER... I'M VERY FAMOUS AND I PLAY FOR ENGLAND?
!
THAT SHOULD DO NICELY.
THOUGHT SO.

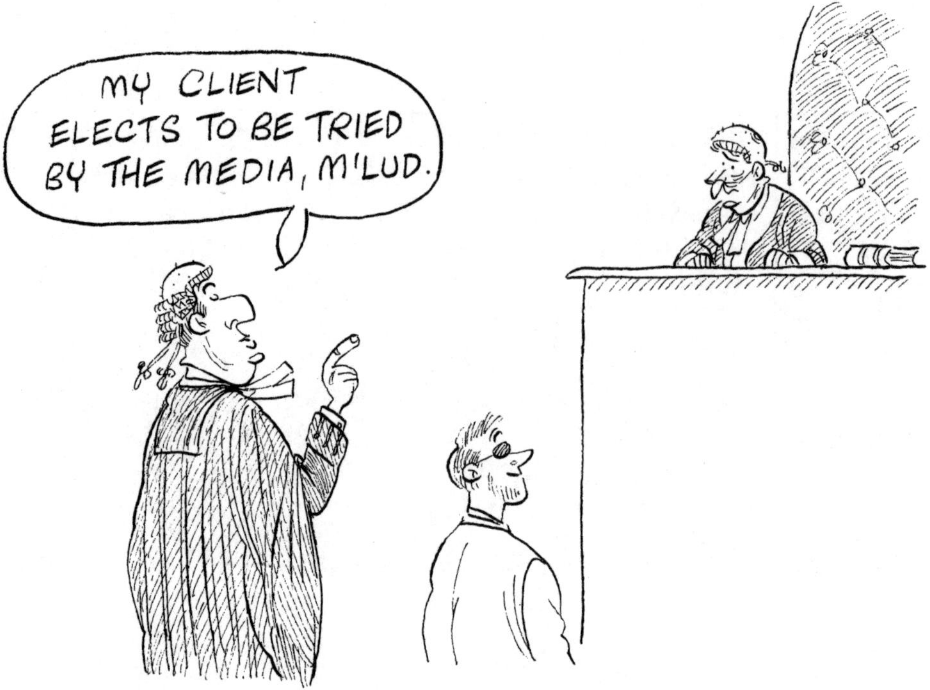
MY CLIENT ELECTS TO BE TRIED BY THE MEDIA, M'LUD.

I PROMISE TO TELL THE TRUTH, THE WHOLE TRUTH, AND NOTHING BUT THE TRUTH.

AS FAR AS I CAN REMEMBER IT

WE PROMISE TO TELL EVASIONS AND HALF-TRUTHS, WITHOUT EVER ACTUALLY TELLING AN UNTRUTH.

I PROMISE TO TRY AND WORK OUT WHICH SIDE IS TELLING THE TRUTH.

I EXERCISE MY RIGHT TO SILENCE AND HOPE NO-ONE FINDS OUT THE REAL TRUTH

DOCTOR, IS IT YOUR EVIDENCE THAT THE CLAIMANT IS A MALINGERER?
WITHOUT A DOUBT.
I CERTAINLY WOULD NOT BE TESTIFYING HERE IF I THOUGHT OTHERWISE.
UNLESS OF COURSE I WAS GIVING EVIDENCE FOR THE OTHER SIDE...
...IN WHICH CASE IT WOULD BE POST-TRAUMATIC STRESS DISORDER.

THIS IS A VERY, SERIOUS CHARGE, YOUNG MAN. YOU MAY NEED A LAWYER TO REPRESENT YOU.
NO, I DON'T. I'M GOING TO TELL THE TRUTH.

Chapter 2
M'Learned Friends

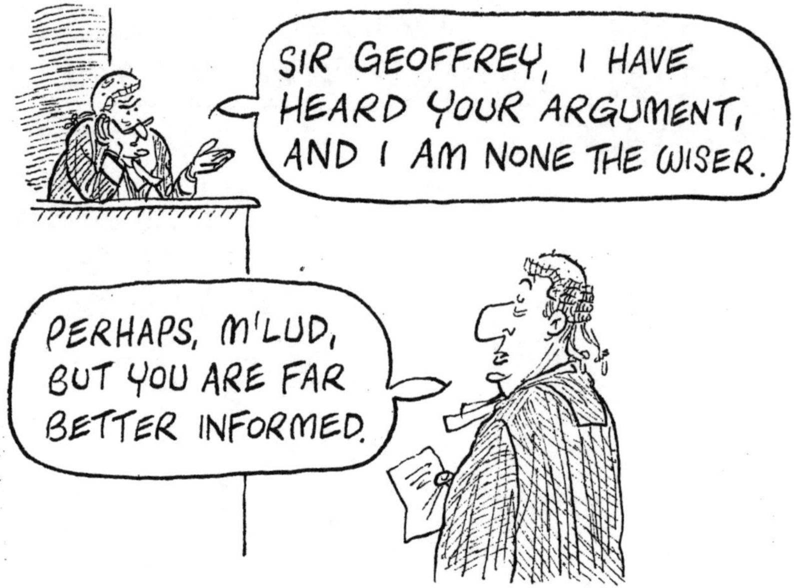
SIR GEOFFREY, I HAVE HEARD YOUR ARGUMENT, AND I AM NONE THE WISER.
PERHAPS, M'LUD, BUT YOU ARE FAR BETTER INFORMED.

WHAT IS THE COLLECTIVE NOUN FOR LAWYERS, SIR GEOFFREY? ARE WE A FLOCK OR A PRIDE?
A RAMPAGE, PERHAPS? AN EVASION... OF TAX LAWYERS?
A SCHOOL? A VERBAGE?
NONE OF THE ABOVE, DEAR BOY.
WE ARE A GLUT.

TRUTH in LAW
SIR GEOFFREY, HOW LONG DO YOU INTEND TO BORE ME WITH THIS CASE?
M'LUD, SINCE I AM ON A DAILY RATE... AS LONG AS POSSIBLE.
AND YOU, MR LONG-WIND?
M'LUD, I TOO SEEK THE MAXIMUM PROLIXITY AND DELAY.
I SEE... AND YOUR DEFENCE? THE USUAL NONSENSE?
A WEB OF HALF-TRUTHS AND EVASIONS.
I'LL PUT YOU DOWN FOR A THREE DAY TRIAL... WAKE ME UP AFTER TWO WEEKS WOULD YOU?
...IF WE HAVEN'T TAKEN A MORE LUCRATIVE CASE BY THEN.

YOUR LORDSHIP WILL BE GLAD TO HEAR THAT I INTEND TO ADVANCE AN ARGUMENT UNCORRUPTED BY ANY LEGAL MERITS.

HARD DAY DEAR?
THE WORST, MOST EGREGIOUS CASE OF ADVERSE POSS-ESSION I HAVE EVER SEEN!
WHAT'S THAT, DEAR?
"SQUATTER'S RIGHTS." THE CLAIMANT LACKS FORMAL TITLE, BUT OCCUPIES THE LAND ANY-WAY.
I SEE, DEAR.
IT'S A SAD DAY WHEN A MAN CAN'T ENJOY HIS OWN PROPERTY IN PEACE.
...BUT WHY DON'T YOU JUST THROW THE DOG OFF THE SOFA IF YOU WANT TO SIT DOWN?
WHO DOES HE THINK RUNS THIS HOUSE ANYWAY?
NN

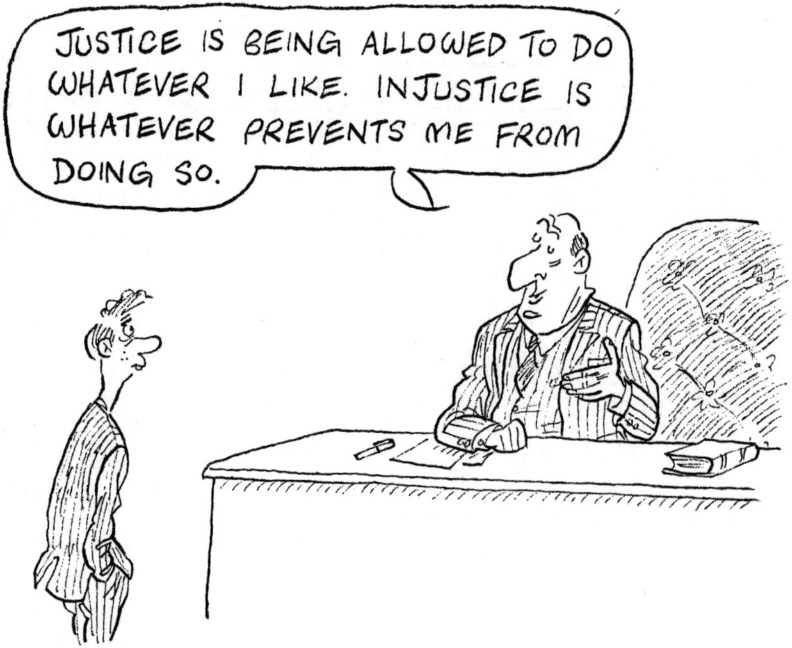
JUSTICE IS BEING ALLOWED TO DO WHATEVER I LIKE. INJUSTICE IS WHATEVER PREVENTS ME FROM DOING SO.

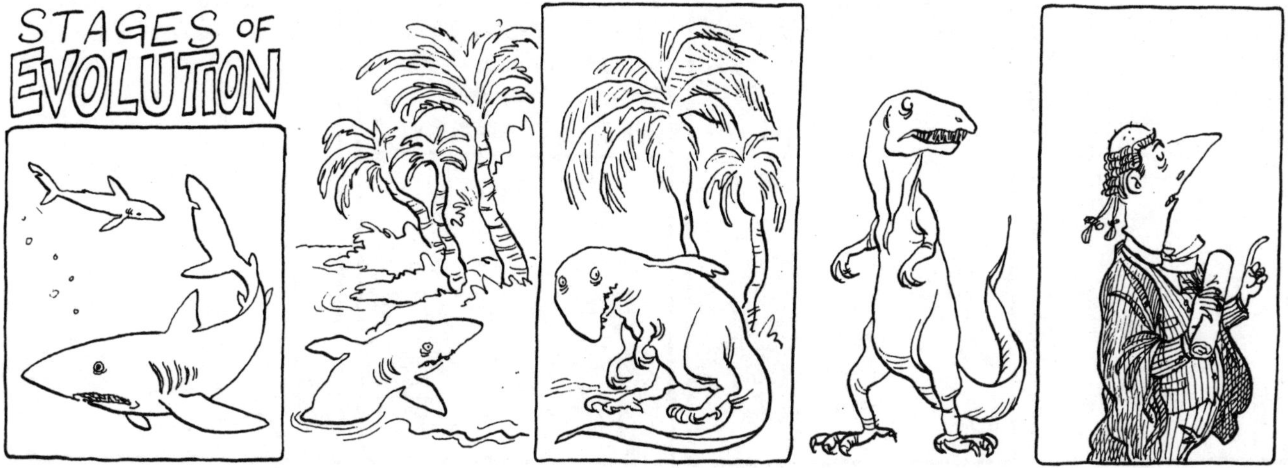
STAGES OF
EVOLUTION

BUT SIR GEOFFREY, DOESN'T IT BOTHER YOU TO DEFEND A MAN WHOM YOU KNOW TO BE GUILTY?
NOT AT ALL
EVERY MAN HAS THE RIGHT TO A PROPER DEFENCE.
BESIDES, UNDER ENGLISH LAW, AND IN THESE CHAMBERS, EVERY DEFENDANT IS PRESUMED INNOCENT.
...UNTIL PROVEN BANKRUPT.

IF LAW WERE LIKE FOOTBALL...
...THERE WOULD BE SENDING-OFF FOR AGGRESSIVE BEHAVIOUR...
Red Card
SHAME
...EMBARRASSINGLY OVER-the-TOP CELEBRATIONS...
...PARTISAN SUPPORT FOR the PLAYERS...
WHO ATE ALL THE PIES?
BULGE
... and BUNGS.
£

MARRIED? YOU'RE FAR TOO YOUNG.
I FORBID IT.
OH, COME ON DADDY.
BUT HE'S SO... UNSUITABLE! NO PROSPECTS, NO PROPER JOB.
THAT'S NOT TRUE!
HE'LL NEVER MAKE ANYTHING OF HIMSELF!
HMF!
MY OWN DAUGHTER, MARRYING THAT... ...THAT...
SOLICITOR!
DON'T BE SO POMPOUS DADDY.

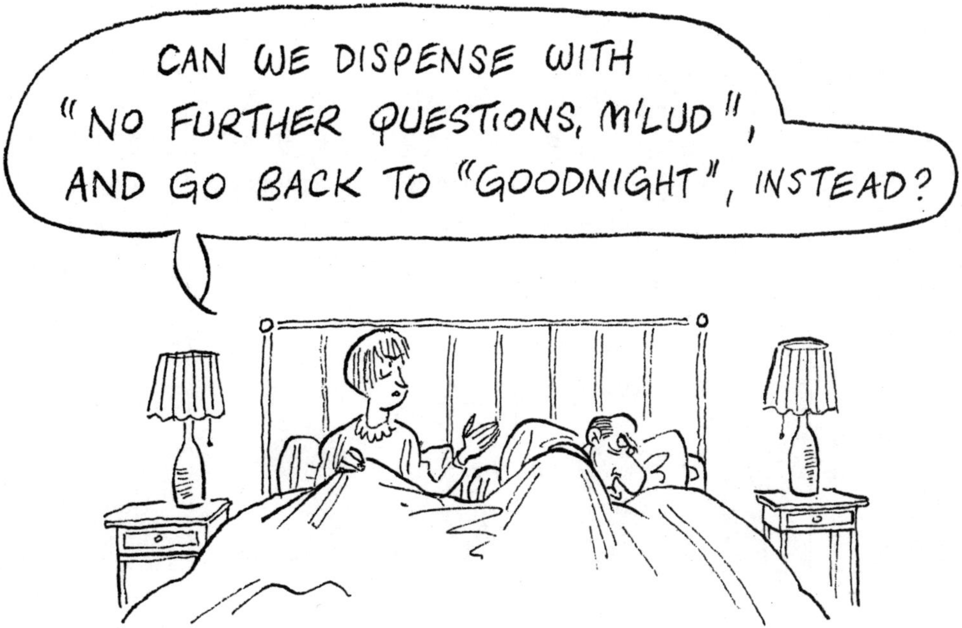
CAN WE DISPENSE WITH "NO FURTHER QUESTIONS, M'LUD", AND GO BACK TO "GOODNIGHT", INSTEAD?

HOW DID YOUR CASE GO?
NOT SO GOOD. I ALWAYS SEEM TO HAVE THE SAME THREE ARGUMENTS.
FIRST, THE ONE I PREPARE THE NIGHT BEFORE: LOGICAL, CLEAR, ORGANISED.
SECOND, THE ONE I ACTUALLY PRESENT ON THE DAY: MUDDLED, DISORGANISED, INCOMPLETE.
...AND FINALLY THE ONE I THINK OF AS SOON AS I LEAVE THE COURTROOM: BRILLIANT, DEVAST-ATING, IRREBUTTABLE.

MEMBERS OF THE BAR, ALTERNATIVE DISPUTE RESOLUTION, OR "ADR", IS HERE TO STAY.
2002 BAR CONFERENCE
A SIMPLE TORTS CLAIM MIGHT TAKE FIVE YEARS AND FIFTY THOUSAND POUNDS TO COME TO TRIAL.
2002 BAR CONFERENCE
ADR PROMISES A QUICK, SIMPLE, EFFICIENT, AND LAWYER-FREE PATH TO JUSTICE.
2002 BAR CONFERENCE
...WHICH IS WHY WE MUST LEARN TO RECOGNISE IT
2002 BAR CONFERENCE
... AND SQUASH IT LIKE A BUG.
2002 BAR CONFERENCE

YOU SOLICITORS ARE ALL THE SAME - ALWAYS WANTING FREE ADVICE ON THE TELEPHONE!
IF YOU WANT COUNSEL'S OPINION YOU CAN SEND ME A BRIEF AND PAY FOR IT LIKE EVERY-ONE ELSE!
...DO I MAKE MYSELF CLEAR?
YOU HAVE TO BE FIRM WITH THESE PEOPLE!
QUITE RIGHT.
OH, AND DAD, TELL MUM I'LL BE LATE FOR LUNCH ON SUNDAY

HOW'S THAT DISPUTE WITH YOUR NEIGHBOUR OVER THE GARDEN HEDGE GOING?
NOT SO GOOD, I'M AFRAID.
BUT I THOUGHT YOU WON THE CASE?
I DID
...AND YOU GOT AN ORDER FOR HIM TO TRIM THE HEDGE?
YES
SO WHAT'S THE PROBLEM?
SNIP! SNIP!
OH... I SEE.

YOU KNOW, SIR ELTON, YOU AND I HAVE MUCH IN COMMON. BOTH OF US ARE STARS IN OUR RESPECTIVE FIELDS.
WE ARE BOTH, IN A SENSE, PERFORMERS. YOU, ON THE STAGE, ME, HERE IN THE HIGH COURT.
... BOTH MASTERS OF LANGUAGE ... WE BOTH ... ER ...
... WEAR WIGS ?

WHERE'S SIR GEOFFREY TODAY?
OH, HE'S SPEAKING AT A RALLY IN SUPPORT OF STRIKING CRIMINAL DEFENCE BARRISTERS.
REALLY?
YES. SOMETHING ABOUT RATES OF PAY FOR LEGAL AID WORK BEING FROZEN.
APPARENTLY THESE STRIKERS ARE QUITE A MILITANT LOT.
WHAT IS IT THAT WE REQUIRE?
MORE MONETARY CONSIDERATION!
WHEN DO WE REQUIRE IT?
PRESENTLY!
EX-WIFE & HOUSE IN COUNTRY TO SUPPORT
KEEP MY KIDS IN PUBLIC SCHOOL

'MORNING SIR GEOFFREY, I'VE GOT A NEW SET OF INSTRUCTIONS FOR YOU.
INDEED?
YOU'VE BEEN ASKED TO REPRESENT THE LONDON UNION OF LAP DANCERS IN AN ACTION AGAINST THEIR EMPLOYERS.
THEY NEED YOU TO VISIT ALL THEIR CLUBS AND COMPILE A REPORT ON THEIR WORKING CONDITIONS.
REALLY?
NO.
APRIL FOOL!

Chapter 3
The Client

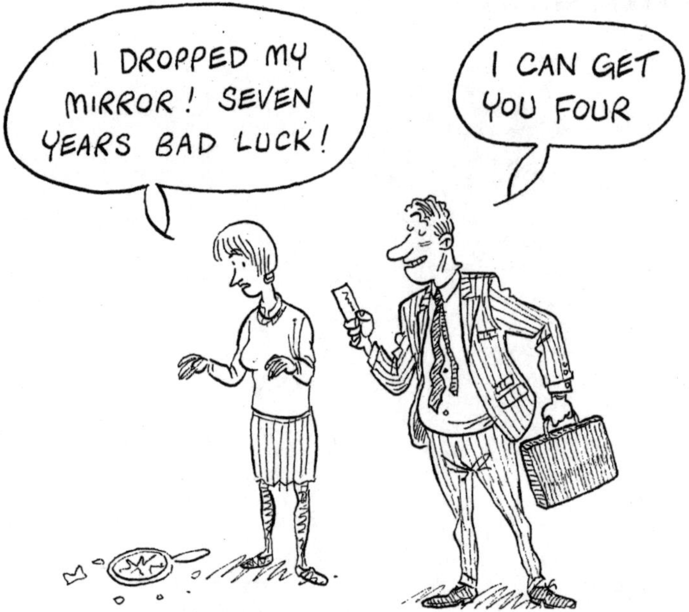
I DROPPED MY MIRROR! SEVEN YEARS BAD LUCK!
I CAN GET YOU FOUR

BEFORE WE WRAP UP THE CONFERENCE, MR SPROCKETT, IS THERE ANYTHING YOU WANT TO ASK?
HOW MUCH WILL YOUR FEE BE?
AHEM... I'M AFRAID I CAN'T DISCUSS FEES. YOU'LL HAVE TO SPEAK TO MY CLERK.
ER... WHAT ARE THE CHANCES OF SUCCESS?
I'M NOT IN THE PREDICTIONS GAME – I CAN'T POSSIBLY SAY AT THIS EARLY STAGE.
WELL, HOW LONG WILL IT TAKE?
IMPOSSIBLE TO SAY.
THANKS FOR COMING IN, MR SPROCKETT. IF THERE IS ANYTHING ELSE YOU WANT TO KNOW, DON'T HESITATE TO CALL YOUR SOLICITOR.

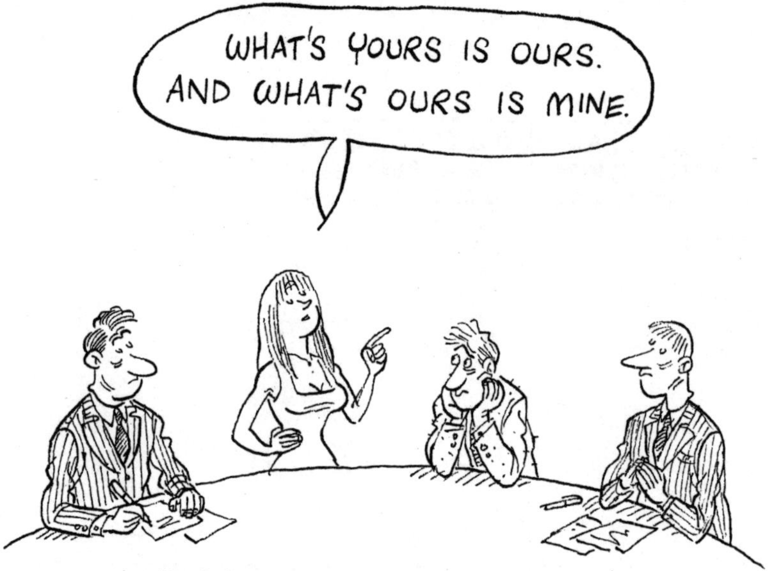
WHAT'S YOURS IS OURS. AND WHAT'S OURS IS MINE.

UNDERSTANDING DIVORCE

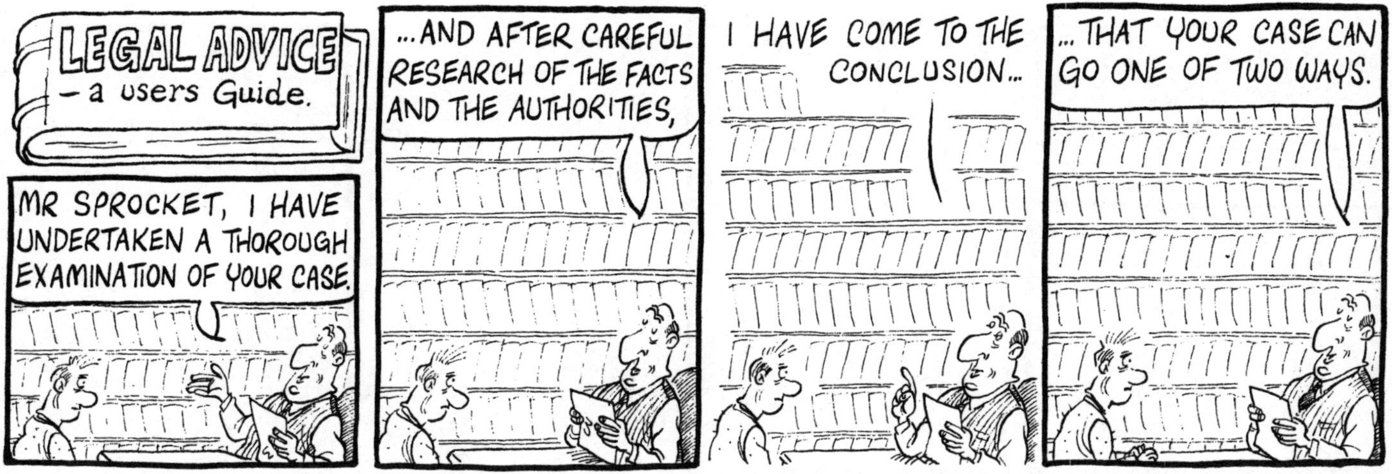
LEGAL ADVICE
– a users Guide.
MR SPROCKET, I HAVE UNDERTAKEN A THOROUGH EXAMINATION OF YOUR CASE.
...AND AFTER CAREFUL RESEARCH OF THE FACTS AND THE AUTHORITIES,
I HAVE COME TO THE CONCLUSION...
...THAT YOUR CASE CAN GO ONE OF TWO WAYS.

SIR GEOFFREY'S GUIDE to DEALING WITH TRICKY LEGAL QUESTIONS
① BE OPTIMISTIC:
MR SPROCKET, YOUR CASE IS A SURE-FIRE WINNER.
② CONSULT AN EXPERT
WHAT AN INTRIGUING QUESTION... AS IT HAPPENS, MY COLLEAGUE HERE IS AN EXPERT ON THAT VERY AREA OF LAW.
③ CALL IN SICK
HELP! MY COUNSEL'S FAINTED!
④ PASS THE BUCK.
...QUITE SO M'LUD. MY LEARNED PUPIL WILL ADDRESS YOU ON THAT VERY POINT.

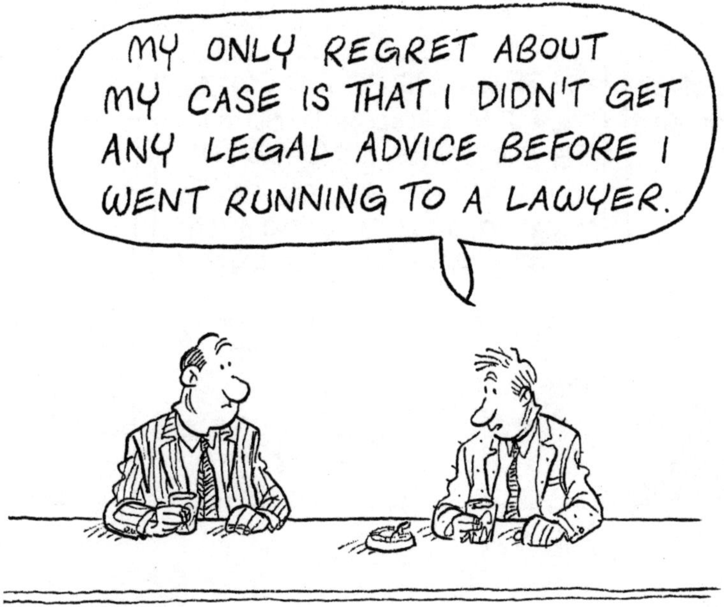
MY ONLY REGRET ABOUT MY CASE IS THAT I DIDN'T GET ANY LEGAL ADVICE BEFORE I WENT RUNNING TO A LAWYER.

...BUT SHOULD I ACCEPT THE OTHER SIDE'S OFFER, SIR GEOFFREY?
THAT DEPENDS
YOU SHOULD ACCEPT THEIR OFFER ONLY IF YOU FEEL SATISFIED THAT THE CHANCES OF SUING AND NOT LOSING ARE NO GREATER THAN THE POSSIBILITY OF NOT SUING AND ACCEPTING AN OFFER WHICH IS NOT HIGH ENOUGH.
IT REALLY IS AS SIMPLE AS THAT, MR SPROCKET

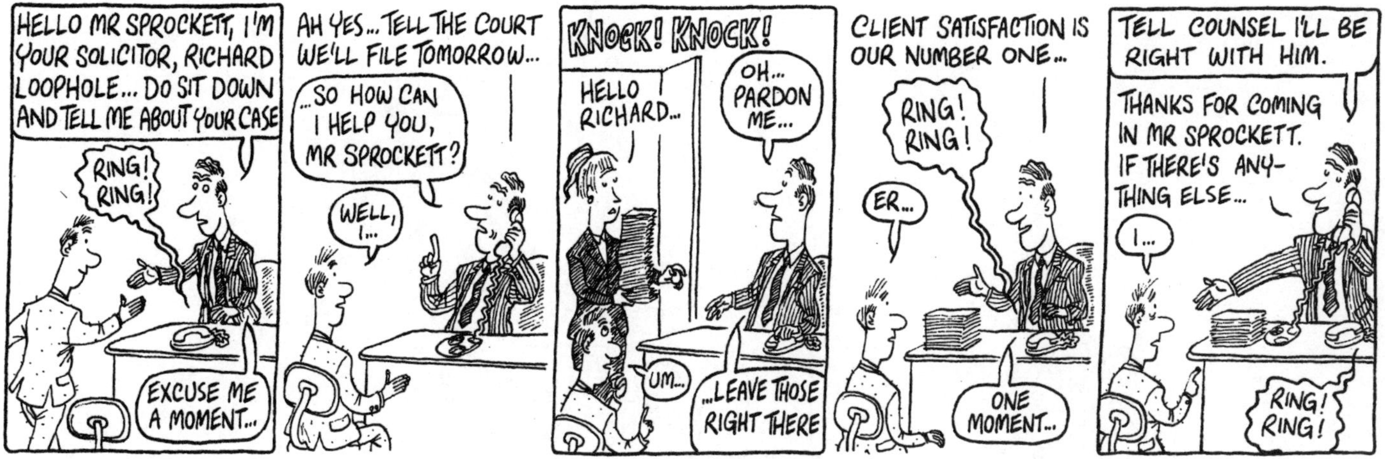
HELLO MR SPROCKETT, I'M YOUR SOLICITOR, RICHARD LOOPHOLE... DO SIT DOWN AND TELL ME ABOUT YOUR CASE
RING! RING!
EXCUSE ME A MOMENT...
AH YES... TELL THE COURT WE'LL FILE TOMORROW...
...SO HOW CAN I HELP YOU, MR SPROCKETT?
WELL, I...
KNOCK! KNOCK!
HELLO RICHARD...
OH... PARDON ME...
UM...
...LEAVE THOSE RIGHT THERE
CLIENT SATISFACTION IS OUR NUMBER ONE...
RING! RING!
ER...
ONE MOMENT...
TELL COUNSEL I'LL BE RIGHT WITH HIM.
THANKS FOR COMING IN MR SPROCKETT. IF THERE'S ANY-THING ELSE...
I...
RING! RING!

TALK IS CHEAP, MR SPROCKET.
BUT NOT AT THIS FIRM...

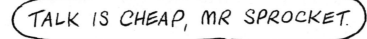

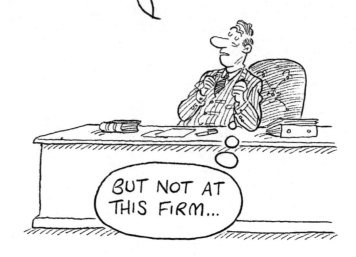

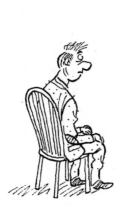

EVER SINCE MY HUSBAND DIED THERE'S BEEN NO END OF TROUBLE WITH HIS ESTATE!
MEETINGS WITH SOLICITORS, LETTERS, PAPERS, OPINIONS FROM COUNSEL, CONFERENCES..
...FEES, LITIGATION, EXPENSES, BRIEFS, COURT HEARINGS, MORE FEES... I DON'T KNOW WHAT!
SOMETIMES IT MAKES ME WISH HE HADN'T DIED!

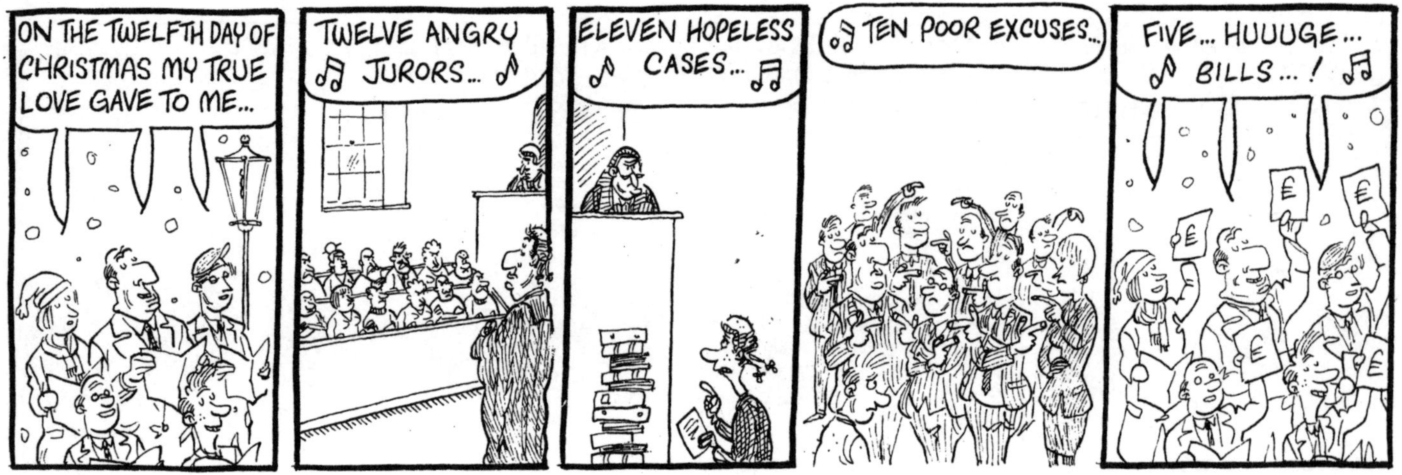
ON THE TWELFTH DAY OF CHRISTMAS MY TRUE LOVE GAVE TO ME...
TWELVE ANGRY JURORS...
ELEVEN HOPELESS CASES...
TEN POOR EXCUSES...
FIVE... HUUUGE... BILLS...!
£
£
£
£
£

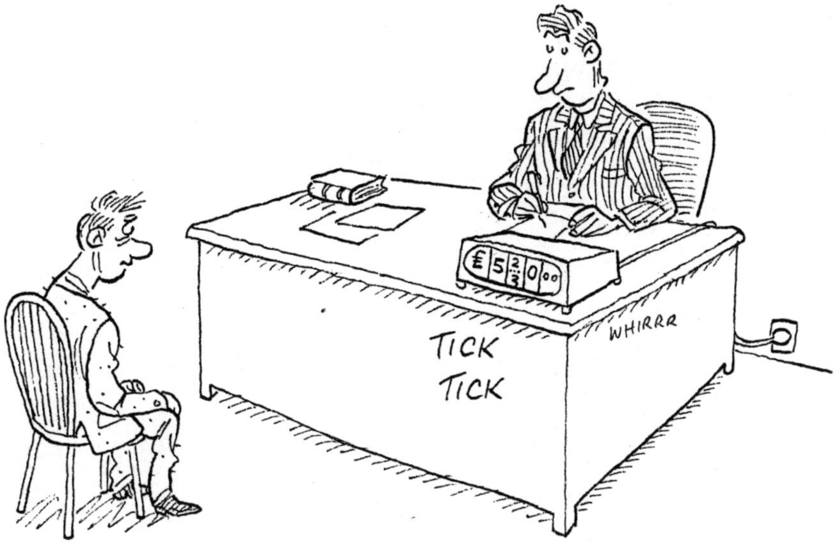

WHIRRR
TICK
TICK

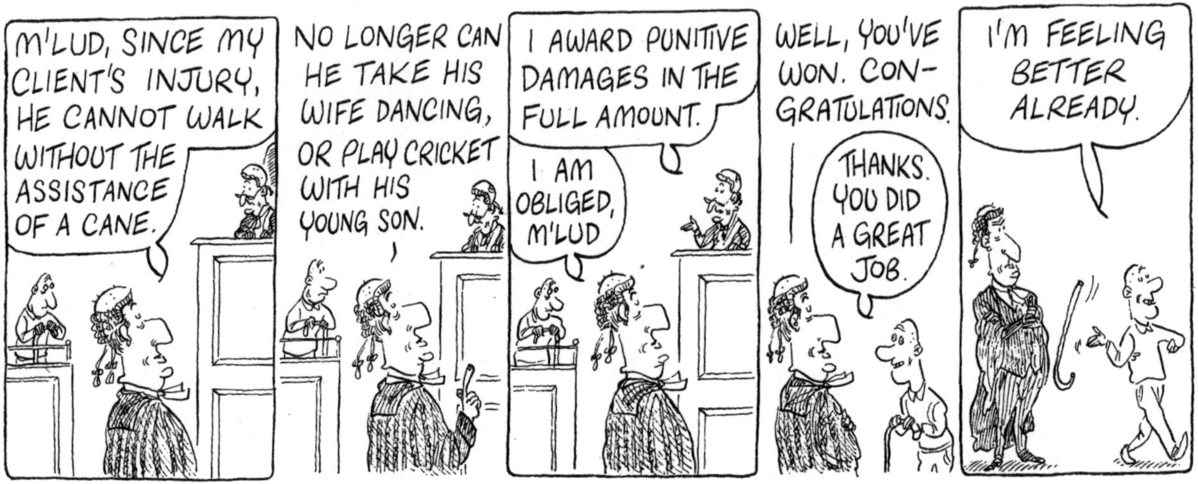

M'LUD, SINCE MY CLIENT'S INJURY, HE CANNOT WALK WITHOUT THE ASSISTANCE OF A CANE.
NO LONGER CAN HE TAKE HIS WIFE DANCING, OR PLAY CRICKET WITH HIS YOUNG SON.
I AWARD PUNITIVE DAMAGES IN THE FULL AMOUNT.
I AM OBLIGED, M'LUD
WELL, YOU'VE WON. CON-GRATULATIONS.
THANKS. YOU DID A GREAT JOB.
I'M FEELING BETTER ALREADY.

Chapter 4
On the Bench

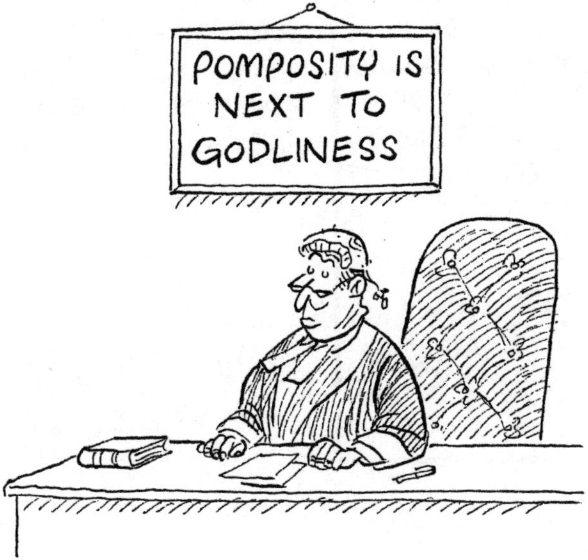
POMPOSITY IS NEXT TO GODLINESS

SO WE'RE GETTING A US-STYLE SUPREME COURT AFTER ALL
...AND LOOK... THEY EVEN FOUND A VENUE.
SUPREME COURT -SITE CHOSEN AT LAST
WHAT WE NEED IS A BUILDING THAT CAPTURES THE ESSENCE OF WHAT JUSTICE IN THIS COUNTRY IS ALL ABOUT.
...SOMETHING THAT PROCLAIMS THE TRUE SPIRIT OF THE LEGAL SYSTEM.
...ARE YOU SURE THIS IS THE RIGHT PLACE?
NATIONAL LOTTERY HEADQUARTERS
SOLD FOR RE-DEVEL-OPMENT

I JUST DON'T KNOW HOW TO JUDGE THIS CASE. BOTH SIDES HAVE GOOD ARGUMENTS, AND THE WITNESSES ALL SOUND CONVINCING.
JUDGE'S CHAMBERS
HOW WOULD YOU DECIDE IT?
WELL... LET ME SEE THE WRITTEN SUBMISSIONS.
HMM... YES... JUST AS I THOUGHT.
WHAT?!
A TYPO. I GENERALLY FIND FOR THE PARTY WITH THE FEWEST SPELLING ERRORS

I SEE THAT THE BAR COUNCIL HAVE CALLED FOR MORE DIVERSITY IN JUDICIAL APPOINTMENTS.
ETHNIC MINORITIES, WOMEN AND PERSONS WITH DISABILITIES ARE ENCOURAGED TO APPLY.
WELL... THAT'S SIR GEOFFREY DONE FOR THEN.
HMM... NOT NECESSARILY.
HAS ANYONE SEEN MY KORAN?

COURT of APPEAL
DECISIONS TRANSLATED
HAVING EXHAUSTIVELY RESEARCHED THE AUTH-ORITIES...
...WE READ THE SKE-LETON ARGUMENTS.
...AND WITH DUE REGARD TO THE TRUE INTENT OF THE LEGISLATION...
...WE MAKE OUR OWN LAW AROUND HERE.
...AND WHILE GIVING GREAT WEIGHT TO THE FINDINGS OF THE LEARNED JUDGE BELOW...
...THE TWIT WHO MADE A MESS OF THIS TRIAL.
...A FAIR READING OF THE TESTIMONY ESTABLISHED...
THIS IS WHAT WE THINK HAPPENED...
...THAT DESPITE PROCEDURAL ERRORS, THE DEFENDANT SUFF-ERED NO PREJUDICIAL EFFECT.
HE'S AS GUILTY AS HELL ANYWAY.

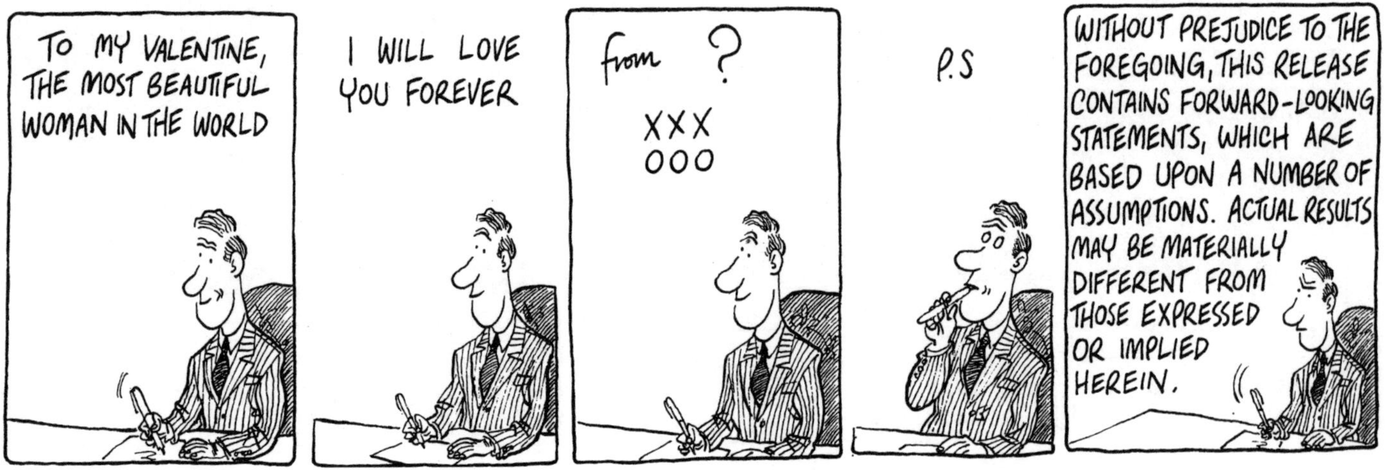
TO MY VALENTINE, THE MOST BEAUTIFUL WOMAN IN THE WORLD
I WILL LOVE YOU FOREVER
from ?
XXX
OOO
P.S
WITHOUT PREJUDICE TO THE FOREGOING, THIS RELEASE CONTAINS FORWARD-LOOKING STATEMENTS, WHICH ARE BASED UPON A NUMBER OF ASSUMPTIONS. ACTUAL RESULTS MAY BE MATERIALLY DIFFERENT FROM THOSE EXPRESSED OR IMPLIED HEREIN.

CIRCUIT JUDGES

SIGH !!
WHO IS TELLING THE TRUTH? CLAIMANT OR DEFENDANT?
ALL THE WITNESSES DISAGREE... THE AUTHORITIES ARE IN CONFLICT...
...THERE'S NOTHING FOR IT BUT TO SEEK EXPERT ASSISTANCE
USHER!
PRESS
YES, JUDGE?
THE COURT IS IN NEED OF EXPERT OPINION
THAT CLAIMANT IS A DIRTY LIAR. I CAN TELL BY HIS SHIFTY LOOKS
I SEE... JUDGEMENT FOR THE DEFENDANT THEN.
...AND COSTS.
...AND COSTS ON THE STANDARD SCALE.

THIS COURT HAS BEEN CHOSEN TO PILOT THE VERY LATEST IN CASE-MANAGEMENT TECHNOLOGY.
PLIK
IN FRONT OF EACH OF YOU IS A SCREEN, ENABLING YOU TO VIEW TRIAL DOCUMENTS IN REAL TIME, WITHOUT THE NEED FOR COUNTLESS PAPER COPIES.
PLIK PLIK
PLOK
THE WHOLE SYSTEM TOOK SIX MONTHS TO INSTALL AND COST OVER €50,000.
SHAKE
SQUEAK
...AND THIS IS MY FIVE YEAR OLD GRANDSON WHO WILL SHOW US ALL HOW TO TURN IT ON.

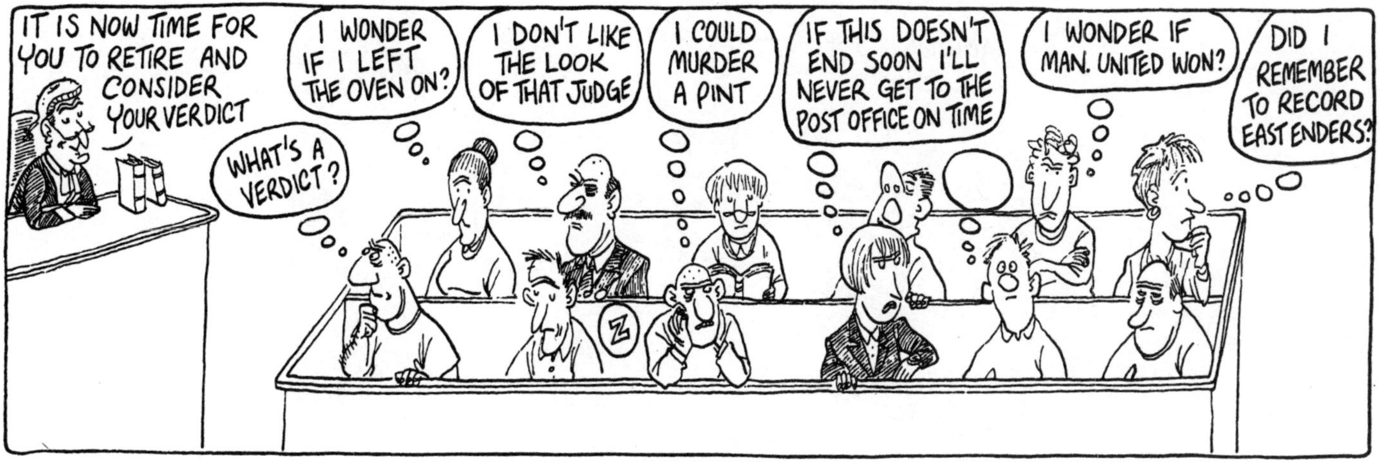
IT IS NOW TIME FOR YOU TO RETIRE AND CONSIDER YOUR VERDICT
WHAT'S A VERDICT?
I WONDER IF I LEFT THE OVEN ON?
I DON'T LIKE THE LOOK OF THAT JUDGE
Z
I COULD MURDER A PINT
IF THIS DOESN'T END SOON I'LL NEVER GET TO THE POST OFFICE ON TIME
I WONDER IF MAN. UNITED WON?
DID I REMEMBER TO RECORD EAST ENDERS?

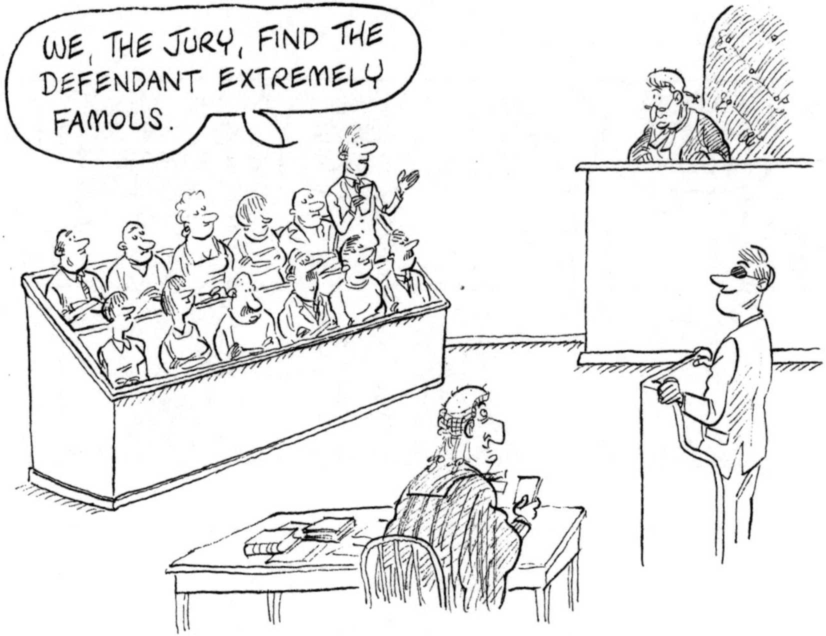
WE, THE JURY, FIND THE DEFENDANT EXTREMELY FAMOUS.

EVERY
DAY IS
JUDGEMENT
DAY

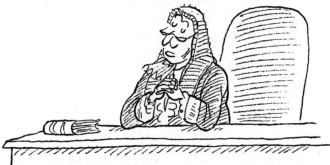

Chapter 5
The Firm

AH... THANK GOD IT'S FRIDAY... I CAN HARDLY BELIEVE IT!
NO PHONE CALLS, CASES, OR CLIENTS FOR TWO WHOLE DAYS!
I'VE GOT ALL OF SATURDAY AND SUNDAY AT HOME...
...TO CATCH UP ON MY BACKLOG OF WORK BEFORE MONDAY MORNING.

WELL, TODAY IS THE THIRTIETH ANNIVERSARY OF MY JOINING THE FIRM.
WHAT DO YOU HAVE THERE? A LETTER OF CONGRATULATIONS?
NO, EVEN BETTER.
FULL EQUITY PARTNERSHIP?
BETTER THAN THAT.
A GOLD WATCH?
BETTER.
...A LETTER FROM MY BANK SAYING I'VE FINALLY PAID OFF MY STUDENT LOANS.

MORE LAWYER'S PSYCHIATRIC DISORDERS
SCHIZOPHRENIA
WE WON THE CASE!
I'M A GENIUS!
WE LOST! I'M A FAILURE!
PEDANTIC OBSESSIVENESS
EVERYTHING IRRELEVANT TO THE CASE NEEDS TO BE FILED IN ALPHABETICAL ORDER.
LITIGATION WITHDRAWAL PARANOIA
DID I REMEMBER TO FILE THE PLEADINGS ON TIME?
IS MY ASSISTANT COPING AT THE OFFICE?
WORKAHOLICISM
LAST NIGHT ONE OF MY TEAM DIED OF OVERWORK
WOW! WHAT A TEAM PLAYER!
WHAT COMMITTMENT!

WHERE ARE YOU GOING ON HOLIDAY THIS YEAR? BACK TO TUSCANY?
YES, WITH EDWARD AND HIS FAMILY.
HM. YOU TWO GET ON WELL, CONSIDERING YOU WORK TOGETHER IN THE SAME DEPARTMENT.
OH... WE'VE BEEN GOING ON HOLIDAY TOGETHER FOR YEARS.
CLICK!
I COULDN'T IMAGINE GOING WITHOUT HIM NOW.
IT'S THE ONLY WAY I CAN STOP HIM STEALING MY CLIENTS WHILE I'M AWAY.

AS YOUR FIRM'S TIME MANAGEMENT CONSULTANT, I HAVE PREPARED A PERSONALISED PROGRAM ON HOW TO USE YOUR TIME MORE EFFICIENTLY
YOU HAVE TWO OPTIONS
THE FIRST OPTION IS TO MAKE YOURSELF AVAIL-ABLE TO YOUR CLIENTS 24 HOURS A DAY.
HERE'S YOUR PAGER -REMEMBER NEVER TO TURN IT OFF.
CANCEL YOUR GOLF CLUB SUBSCRIPTION AND YOUR REGULAR TABLE AT THE LAW SOCIETY.
...AND EAT A SANDWICH AT YOUR DESK INSTEAD.
...AND THE SECOND OPTION ?
DELEGATE ALL YOUR WORK TO YOUR ASSISTANT.
NOW YOU'RE MAKING SENSE

REVENUES ARE DOWN, EXPENSES ARE UP. CAN'T WE GET OUR ASSOCIATES TO WORK HARDER?
BUT THEY WORK INSANE HOURS AS IT IS.
ONE PASSED OUT AT HIS DESK FROM OVERWORK ONLY LAST WEEK!
WELL, LET'S FIRE SOME THEN IF THEY CAN'T TAKE THE PACE!
NO... ALL THAT WOULD DO IS DECREASE OUR BILLINGS...
WELL THERE MUST BE SOME WAY WE CAN SQUEEZE MORE WORK OUT OF THEM.
LIKE HOW?
WHISPER
GREAT IDEA! LET'S DO IT!
ALRIGHT CRAWLEY, YOU'VE HAD YOUR THREE MINUTES – TIME'S UP
TIME IS MONEY
I'LL BE RIGHT WITH YOU!

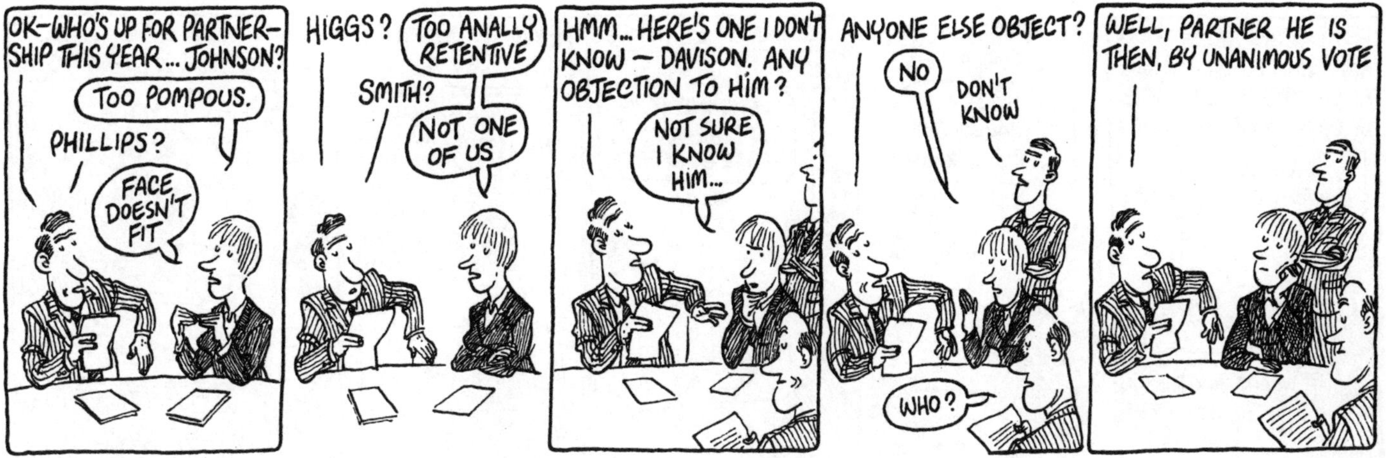
OK–WHO'S UP FOR PARTNERSHIP THIS YEAR... JOHNSON?
TOO POMPOUS.
PHILLIPS?
FACE DOESN'T FIT
HIGGS?
TOO ANALLY RETENTIVE
SMITH?
NOT ONE OF US
HMM... HERE'S ONE I DON'T KNOW – DAVISON. ANY OBJECTION TO HIM?
NOT SURE I KNOW HIM...
ANYONE ELSE OBJECT?
NO
DON'T KNOW
WHO?
WELL, PARTNER HE IS THEN, BY UNANIMOUS VOTE

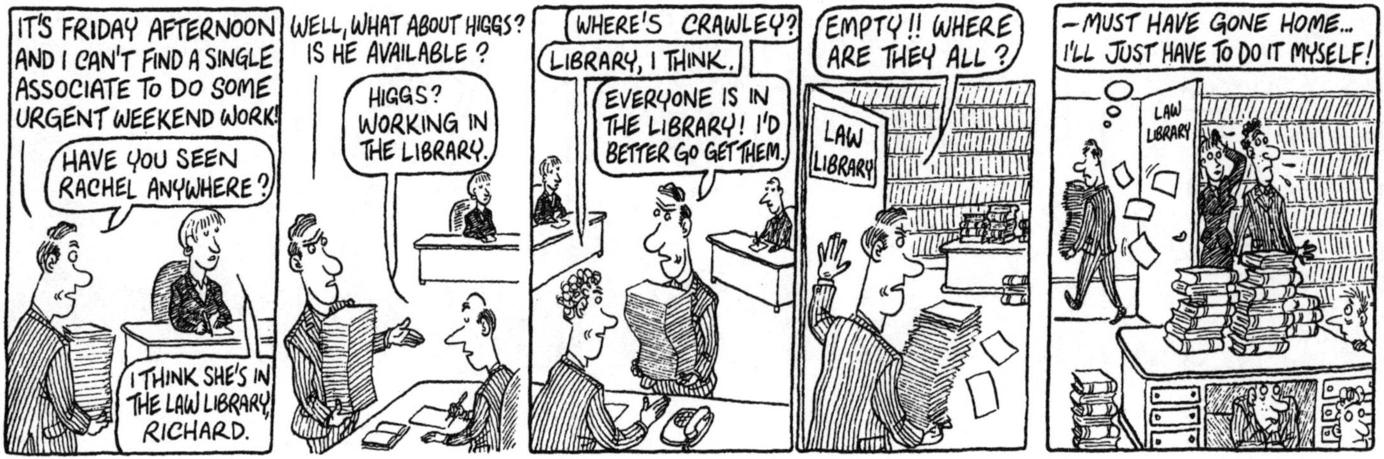

IT'S FRIDAY AFTERNOON AND I CAN'T FIND A SINGLE ASSOCIATE TO DO SOME URGENT WEEKEND WORK!
HAVE YOU SEEN RACHEL ANYWHERE?
I THINK SHE'S IN THE LAW LIBRARY, RICHARD.
WELL, WHAT ABOUT HIGGS? IS HE AVAILABLE?
HIGGS? WORKING IN THE LIBRARY.
WHERE'S CRAWLEY?
LIBRARY, I THINK.
EVERYONE IS IN THE LIBRARY! I'D BETTER GO GET THEM.
LAW LIBRARY
EMPTY!! WHERE ARE THEY ALL?
– MUST HAVE GONE HOME... I'LL JUST HAVE TO DO IT MYSELF!
LAW LIBRARY

AS YOUR RECRUITMENT CONSULTANT, I MUST ADVISE YOU THAT COMPETITION FOR THE TOP LAW GRADUATES WILL BE VERY TOUGH THIS YEAR.
YOU WILL NEED TO PROJECT POSITIVE ATTRIBUTES TO DESCRIBE YOUR FIRM AND YOURSELVES.
OUTSTANDING VIGOROUS EFFECTIVE RESPONSIBLE
POWERFUL AGGRESSIVE INDUSTRIOUS DYNAMIC
AS AN AID TO MEMORY, YOU MAY FIND IT USEFUL TO MEMORISE THE FIRST LETTERS OF THE ABOVE.

OH YES, LOTS OF WORK, MUM. THE BRIEFS JUST FLOOD IN.
...HARDLY A LET-UP REALLY. IT'S ONE CASE AFTER ANOTHER.
MUST DASH. THAT'LL BE ONE OF MY CLIENTS NOW.
KNOCK! KNOCK!
SIGH!
HOOVER
WHHIRRRR

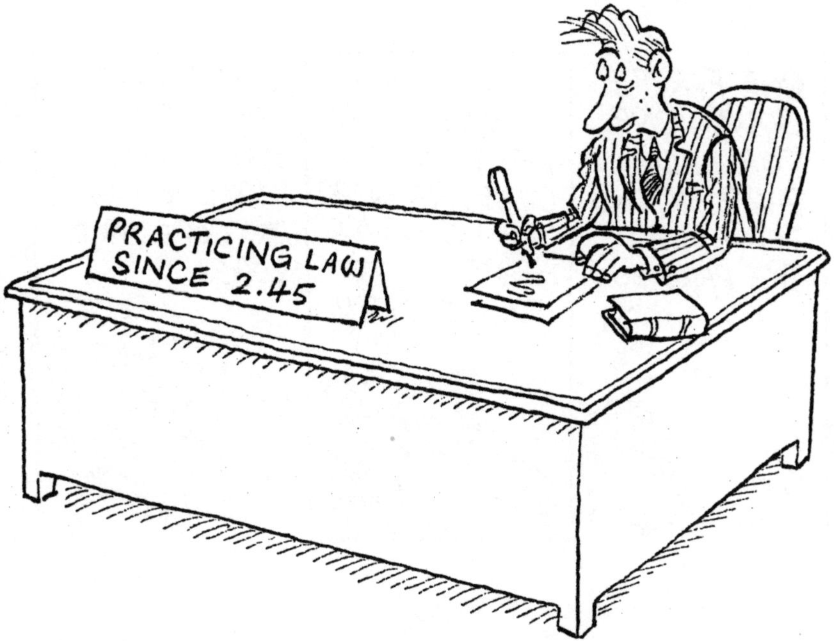
PRACTICING LAW
SINCE 2.45

LET'S SEE... ONE COPY OF THE LITIGATION DOCUMENTS FOR ME... THREE COPIES FOR FILING...
WHIRRR
ONE FOR THE COURT, ONE FOR EACH PARTNER, ONE FOR EACH OF THE PARTIES...
COPY GRIND
CLIENT COPIES, SERVICE COPIES, FIRM COPIES, COPIES FOR EVERY-ONE I'VE NEVER HEARD OF...
WHIRR COPY
COPIES FOR AN EMERGENCY, COPIES FOR ARCHIVE, COPIES AND COPIES AND COPIES AND COPIES...
COPY WHIRRR
HAVE YOU SEEN RACHEL ANYWHERE? SHE WAS HERE COPYING A FEW HOURS AGO...

OFFICER, WHEN YOU FIRST SAW MY CLIENT, HE HAD CROSSED THE CENTRE LINE, SO YOU PULLED HIM OVER?
YES.
...AND YOU SMELLED ALCOHOL ON HIS BREATH?
YES
BUT APART FROM THAT, WAS THERE ANY EVIDENCE THAT HE WAS DRIVING UNDER THE INFLUENCE OF ALCOHOL?
WELL...
HE WASN'T WEARING ANY TROUSERS AND HIS BOXER SHORTS WERE ON HIS HEAD.
CRAWLEY DEAR BOY, NEVER ASK THE WITNESS A QUESTION TO WHICH YOU DON'T ALREADY KNOW THE ANSWER.

CRAWLEY, IF YOU CAN'T CONVINCE THEM, CONFUSE THEM.

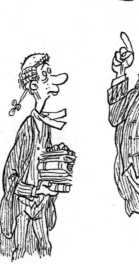

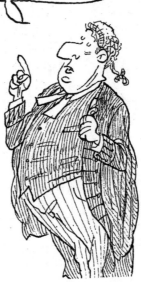

SO LET'S SEE... WHO'S UP FOR TENANCY IN CHAMBERS THIS YEAR ? I HEAR HELENA'S PAPERWORK IS GOOD.
FLAWLESS.
MARVELLOUS ADVOCATE, TOO
I'D SAY SHE'S THE MOST PROMISING PUPIL CHAMBERS HAS HAD IN YEARS.
WITHOUT A DOUBT
I SEE. HIGH PRAISE INDEED.
...WELL THAT LEAVES US WITH NO CHOICE THEN, DOES IT ?
NOT REALLY.
WE'LL HAVE TO GET RID OF HER.
...CAN'T HAVE HER MAKING US LOOK BAD.
—PINCHING OUR WORK

Chapter 6
Legal Ethics

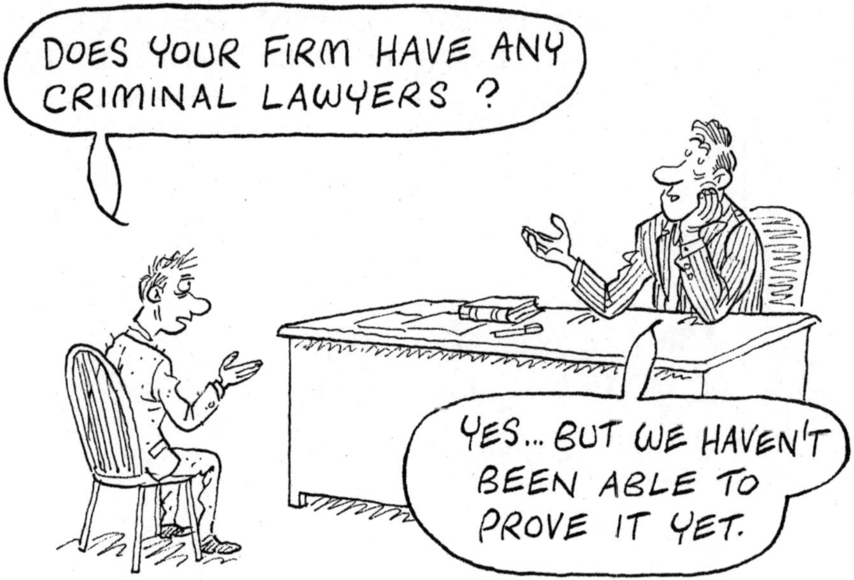
DOES YOUR FIRM HAVE ANY CRIMINAL LAWYERS ?
YES... BUT WE HAVEN'T BEEN ABLE TO PROVE IT YET.

WELL MR SPROCKET, YOU'VE WON YOUR CASE, BUT I'M AFRAID IT'S SOMETHING OF A PYRRHIC VICTORY.
AFTER DISBURSEMENTS, RETAINERS, COSTS, FEES, AND COURT EXPENSES, YOU WILL RECEIVE NOTHING.
NOTHING AT ALL?!?
BUT THEN... WHAT GOOD HAS ALL OF THIS DONE ME?
YOU HAVE BEEN A GOOD CLIENT TO ME MR SPROCKET.
...BUT I MUST SAY YOU SHOW A SURPRISING IGNORANCE OF THE PURPOSES OF LITIGATION

WHAT'S THE CERTIFICATE, RICHARD?
OH... SOME AWARD I GOT FROM THE LAW SOCIETY.
REALLY? LET'S SEE... "THE JOHN GRISHAM AWARD FOR BEST WORK OF LEGAL FICTION."
WOW! I'M IMPRESSED! I DIDN'T KNOW YOU HAD WRITTEN A NOVEL!
NOT A NOVEL.
IT'S FOR MY TIMESHEETS.

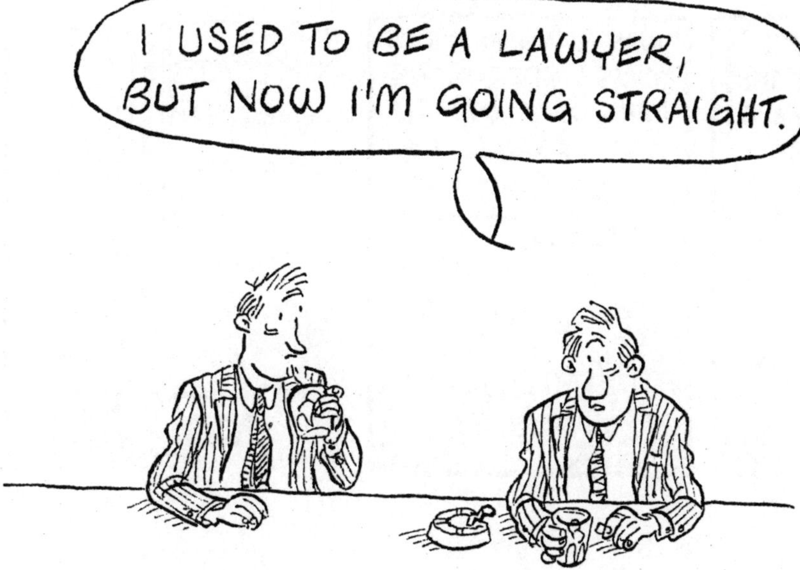
I USED TO BE A LAWYER, BUT NOW I'M GOING STRAIGHT.

I'M SORRY RICHARD, BUT THIS IS ONE OF THE WEAKEST CASES I HAVE EVER COME ACROSS.
REALLY? HOW DISAPPOINTING.
I WAS GOING TO INSTRUCT YOU AS LEADER IN THE HIGH COURT AND THE COURT OF APPEAL. NOW I'LL HAVE TO GET SOME-ONE ELSE.
ON REFLECTION, IT DOES APPEAR TO HAVE SOME HIDDEN MERITS...

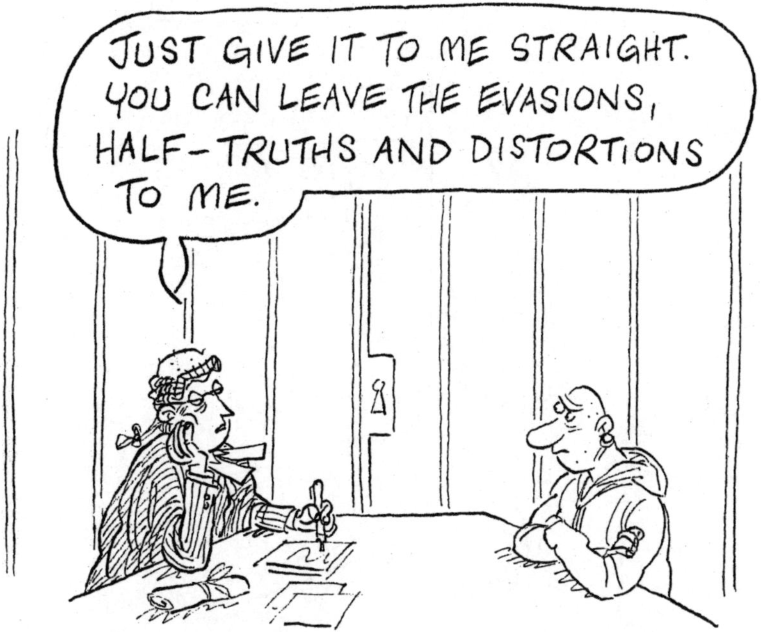
JUST GIVE IT TO ME STRAIGHT. YOU CAN LEAVE THE EVASIONS, HALF-TRUTHS AND DISTORTIONS TO ME.

FICTION
THE HONEST LAWYER
20% OFF

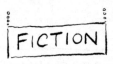

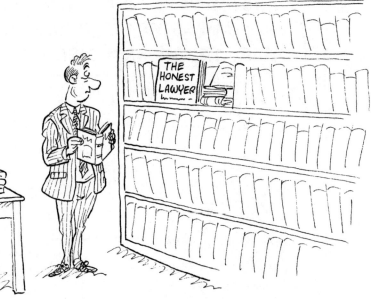

Chapter 7
Legalese

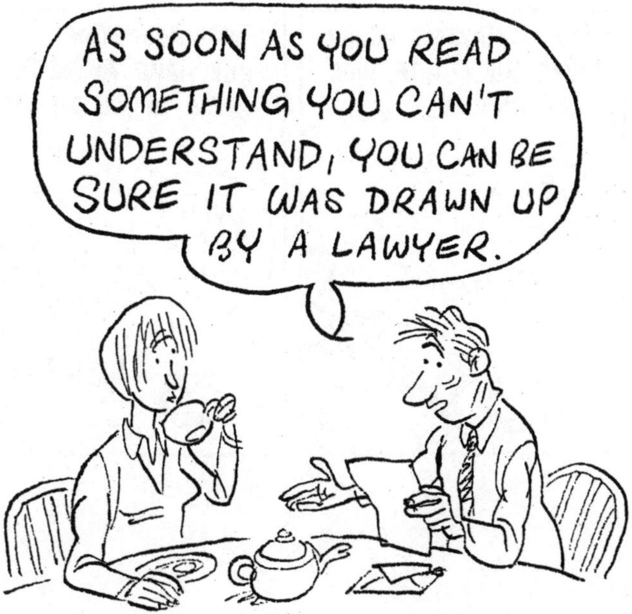
AS SOON AS YOU READ SOMETHING YOU CAN'T UNDERSTAND, YOU CAN BE SURE IT WAS DRAWN UP BY A LAWYER.

HOW TO TRANSLATE LEGALESE
HELLO MR SPROCKET, HOW ARE THINGS ?
GOT ANY NEW BUSINESS FOR ME?
...NO... I HAVEN'T HEARD FROM THE OTHER SIDE LATELY.
RATS. FORGOT TO CALL THEM.
GOOD QUESTION... I'LL HAVE TO GET BACK TO YOU ON THAT.
HAVEN'T GOT A CLUE.
SAY HELLO TO YOUR LOVELY WIFE.
WHAT WAS HER NAME AGAIN ?

LAW-
ENGLISH
DICTIONARY

"BRIEF" (n)

TRANSLATION:
LONG, TIME-CONSUMING
AND EXPENSIVE.

"ABSOLUTELY NOT.
NEVER, EVER."

TRANSLATION:
MY CLIENT WOULD
RATHER NOT CONCEDE
THIS QUITE YET.

"HELLO"

TRANSLATION:
YOUR FIRST
BILLABLE HOUR
HAS JUST BEGUN.

"MONDAY"

TRANSLATION:
HOPEFULLY BY
FRIDAY WEEK, BUT
PROBABLY LATER.

A GUIDE TO LEGAL DRAFTING
NEVER CHOOSE SIMPLE WORDS WHERE COMPLEX ONES WILL ~~DO~~ PROVE REASONABLY PRACTICABLE
NEVER USE ONE DOUBLE NEGATIVE WHERE NO TRIPLE NEGATIVE WILL NOT PROVE UNECESSARY.
MAKE FREE USE OF (a) SUB-PARAGRAPHS, and (b) (i) SUB-SUB-PARAGRAPHS and (ii) SCHEDULES
(SEE ATTACHED SCHEDULE).
THE ONLY DOCUMENT YOUR CLIENT SHOULD BE ABLE TO UNDERSTAND IS YOUR BILL.